English Code 2

Phonics Book

International Phonetic Alphabet (IPA)

IPA SYMBOLS

Consonants

/b/	bag, bike
/d/	desk, opened
/f/	face, free, laugh, photo
/g/	game, good
/h/	hit, hot
/k/	key, kite
/l/	lamp, lucky
/m/	man, monkey
/n/	neck, nut
/ŋ/	ring, flying
/p/	pen, pink
/r/	run, rock
/s/	sun, sell, cycle, grapes
/ʃ/	shirt, shut, shell
/t/	tent, knocked
/θ/	thick, thirsty
/ð/	this, there
/v/	visit, give
/w/	wall, window, what
/ks/	relax, taxi
/j/	yellow, young
/z/	zoo, bananas
/tʃ/	chair, cheese, cheap
/dʒ/	jeans, juice, judge, ginger

Two-Letter Consonant Blend

/bl/	blanket, blue
/pl/	plane, planet
/kl/	clean, climb
/gl/	glass, glove
/fl/	fly, floor
/sl/	sleep, slow
/br/	break, branch
/pr/	price, practice
/kr/	crab
/fr/	fruit
/gr/	grass
/dr/	draw
/tr/	train
/ŋk/	bank, think
/nd/	stand, round
/nt/	student, count
/sk/	scarf, skirt, basket, scary
/sm/	small
/sn/	snow
/sp/	sports, space
/st/	stand, first, stay
/sw/	swim, sweet
/tw/	twelve, twins
/kw/	quick, question

Three-Letter Consonant Blend

/spr/	spring
/str/	street
/skr/	screen
/skw/	square

Vowels

🇺🇸 /ɑː/ 🇬🇧 /ɒ/	top, jog, wash
/æ/	cat, clap, sand
/e/	wet, send, healthy
/ɪ/	hit, sing, pin
/ɔː/	caught, saw, cough
🇺🇸 /ɔːr/ 🇬🇧 /ɔː/	horse, morning
/eɪ/	cake, name, say
/iː/	eat, tree, steam
🇺🇸 /oʊ/ 🇬🇧 /əʊ/	home, coat, snow
/uː/	food, glue, flew, June
/ʌ/	duck, run, cut, honey
/ʊ/	cook, foot, put
🇺🇸 /ər/ 🇬🇧 /ə/	ruler, teacher
/ɜːr/	bird, hurt, word, learn

Diphthongs

/aɪ/	nice, bike
/aʊ/	house, brown
/ɔɪ/	boil, enjoy
🇺🇸 /aːr/ 🇬🇧 /aː/	card, market
🇺🇸 /aɪr/ 🇬🇧 /aɪə/	fire, hire
🇺🇸 /aʊr/, /aʊər/ 🇬🇧 /aʊər/	hour, flower
🇺🇸 /er/ 🇬🇧 /eə/	chair, bear, there
🇺🇸 /ɪr/ 🇬🇧 /ɪə/	near, engineer
/juː/	cute, huge, few

Vowel and Consonant Blend

/ʃən/	station, dictionary
/ɪz/	beaches, bridges
/ɪd/	visited

Contents

1

02 **Listen, point, and repeat.**

1

man

2

pan

3

cap

4

clap

5

cat

6

mat

2  Listen. Then say.

The man with a pan
Can cook eggs and jelly.
That's what the man can do!
That's what the man can do!

3 What other things are there with the same a sound?

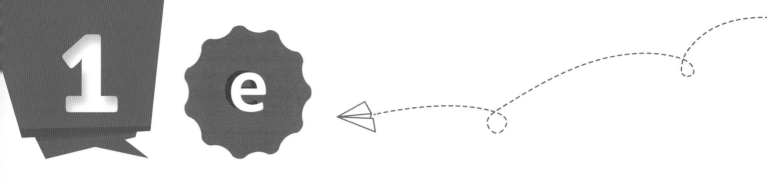

1 e

🎧 04 **Listen, point, and repeat.**

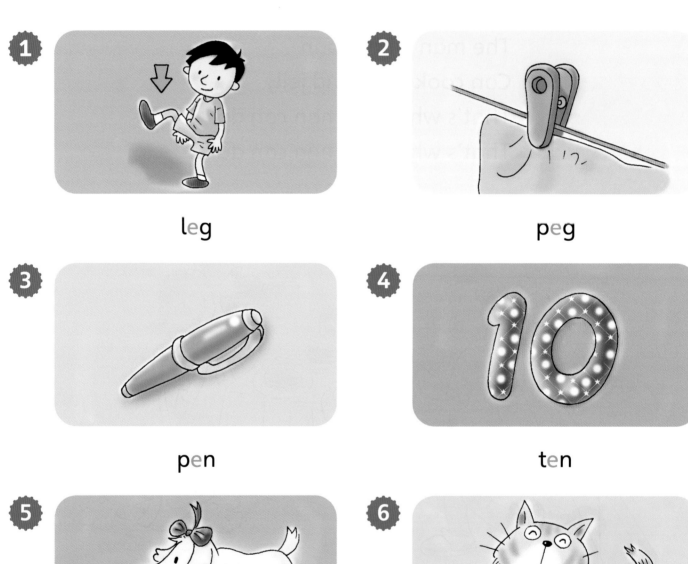

1 leg

2 peg

3 pen

4 ten

5 pet

6 wet

My pet hen in the garden
Gets very wet in the rain.
She gets into bed very fast.
Then she begs to go out again.

My pet ...

6  **Say the chant about your favorite animal.**

2 i

🇺🇸 **American**
trash can

🇬🇧 **British**
bin

1 🎧 06 Listen, point, and repeat.

1

big

2

dig

3

bin

4

sing

5

hit

6
sit

2  Listen. Then say.

Big Tim digging,
Big Tim digging,
Big Tim digging in the mud.
Big Tim digging,
Big Tim digging,
Big Tim digging in the mud.

Big Tim ...

3 What else is Tim doing?
Say another rhyme.

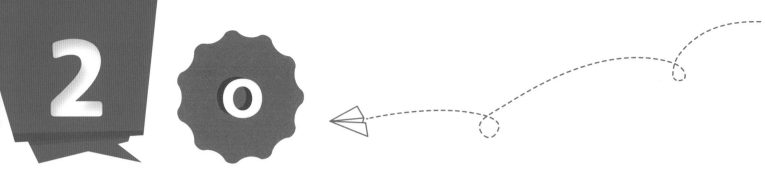

2 o

1   dog

2   jog

3   shop

4   top

5   hot

6   pot

5 🎵 Listen. Then sing.

🇺🇸 American	🇬🇧 British
store	shop

Hop, hop, hop,
All the way to the shop.
I just can't stop,
When I start to hop.

Jog, jog, jog,
On a walk with my dog.
I just can't stop,
When I start to jog.

6 ☀️ Act out the song.

Review 1

1 Play the game. Say the words. Write the missing letters.

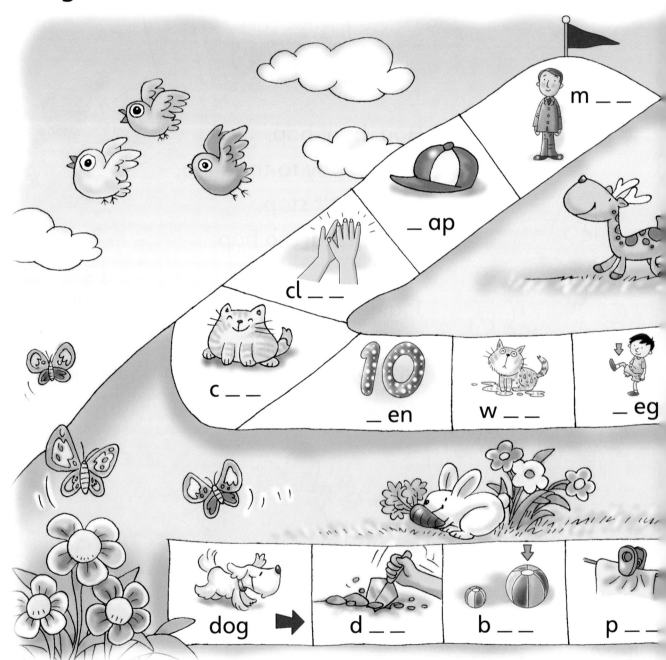

m _ _

_ ap

cl _ _

c _ _

_ en

w _ _

_ eg

dog ➡ d _ _

b _ _

p _ _

s _ _

h _ _

j _ _

_ ot

b _ _

p _ _

p _ _

_ an

_ _ ng

3 u

1 🎧 12 Listen, point, and repeat.

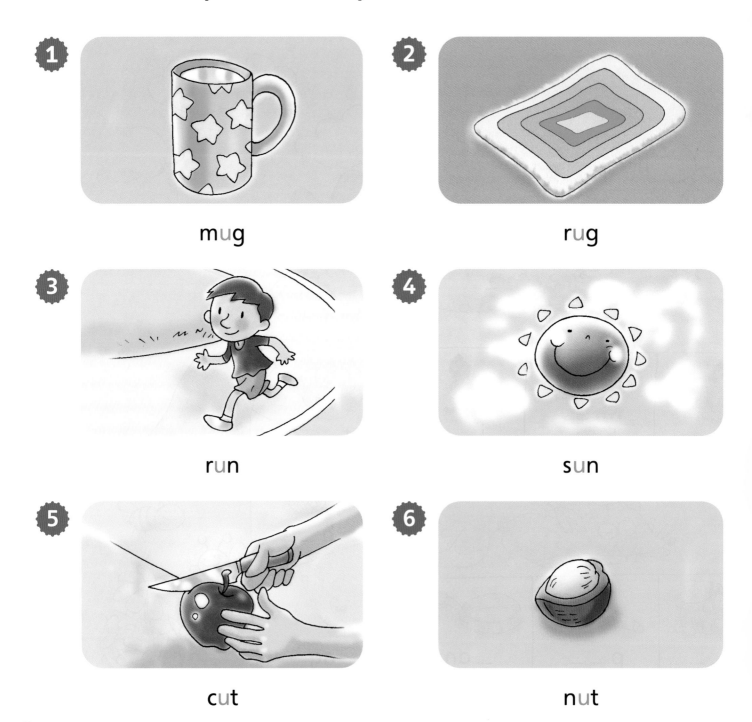

1 mug

2 rug

3 run

4 sun

5 cut

6 nut

2  Listen. Then say.

Give me a hug.
Or sit on the rug.

Walk in the sun.
Or go for a run.

Eat a big nut.
Or live in a hut.

3  Act out what the rats do.

3  **x**

🇺🇸 **American**
ax
🇬🇧 **British**
axe

4 **Listen, point, and repeat.**

 1

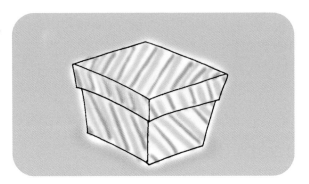

box

2

relax

 3

fox

4

six

5

ax

6

taxi

5  Listen. Then sing.

Give me a box.
Please, please,
Give me a box,
A box for my socks.
Please, please,
Give me a box.

6 What do you put in the box? Sing another song.

4 j

1 🎧 17 **Listen, point, and repeat.**

1

jeans

2

jog

3

jump

4

jacket

5

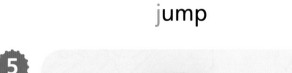

jelly

6

jungle

2 Listen. Then sing.

🇺🇸 American	🇬🇧 British
sweater	jumper

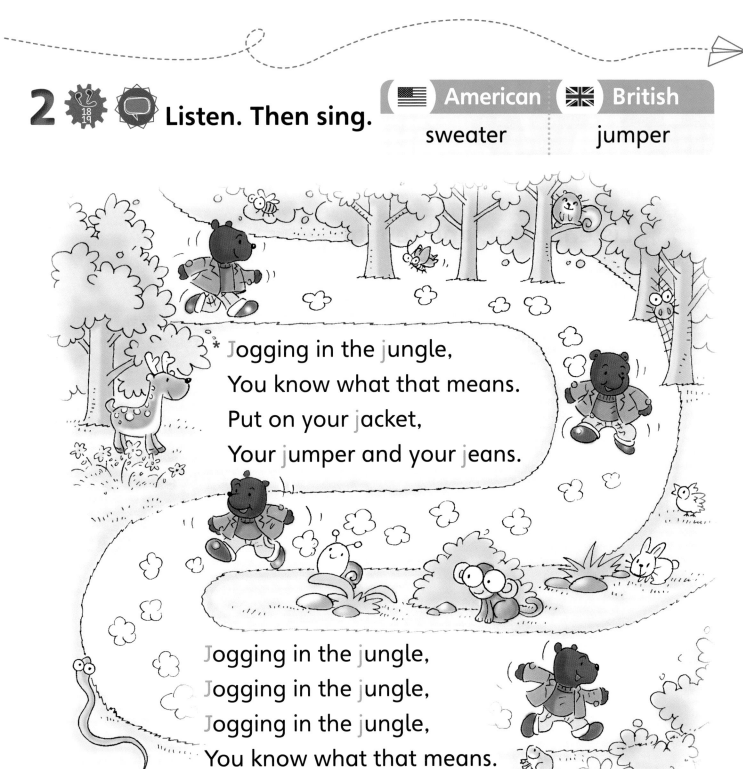

*Jogging in the jungle,
You know what that means.
Put on your jacket,
Your jumper and your jeans.

Jogging in the jungle,
Jogging in the jungle,
Jogging in the jungle,
You know what that means.

* Repeat

3 Your partner goes jogging. What does he/she put on? Sing another song.

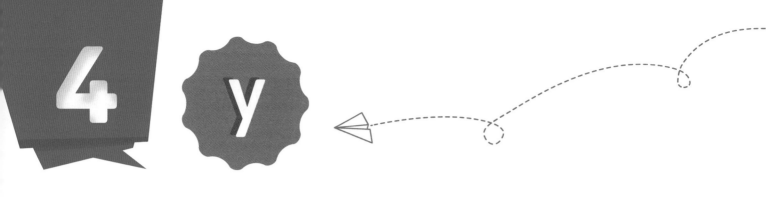

4 — y

4 🎧 20 Listen, point, and repeat.

1

year

2

yes

3

you

4

young

5

yellow

6

yo-yo

5  Listen. Then sing.

Spinning like a yo-yo,
Round and round.
Spinning like a yo-yo,
Round and round.
Yes, it's a yellow yo-yo,
Yes, it's a yellow yo-yo.

6 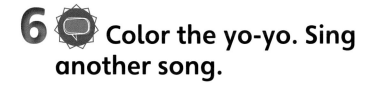 Color the yo-yo. Sing another song.

Review 2

1 Play the game. Say the words. Complete the charts.

Julia   Maxus   Lucy

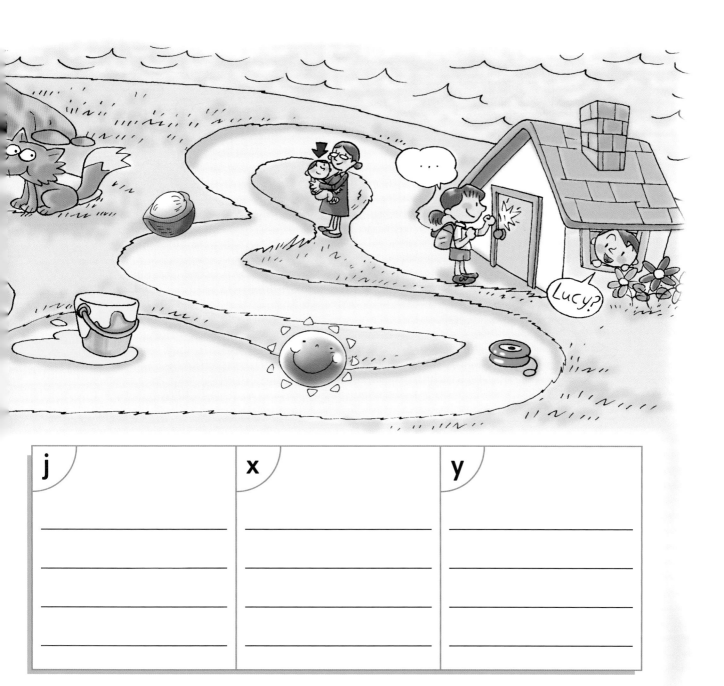

j	x	y

5 ch

🇺🇸 **American**	🇬🇧 **British**
chips	crisps
chili	chilli

1 🎧 24 Listen, point, and repeat.

1

chair

2
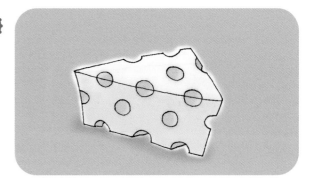
cheese

3

chips

4
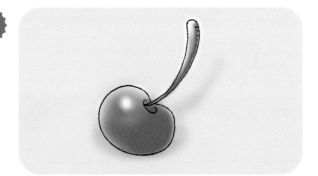
cherry

5

chicken

6

chili

2 🕿 25 💬 Listen. Then say.

Look at the children,
With chips in their hair,
Cheese on their faces,
And sauce on the chairs.

3 💡 What other food is there? Say another chant.

5 sh

4 🎧 Listen, point, and repeat.

1

she

2

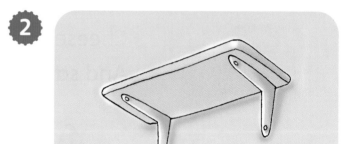

shelf

3

shirt

4

shark

5

short

6

shut

5   Listen and read.

The short lady in the store has a black shirt.

She puts books on the shelf.

She sells books to children.

Then she shuts the door.

May I have ...

6 Work in pairs. Buy things from the store.

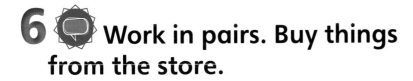

th (1)

1 🎧 28 Listen, point, and repeat.

1

this

2

that

3

these

4

those

5

there

6

they

2  ♫ Listen. Then sing.

Which do you want to play,

This or that, this or that?

Which do you want to play?

This or that, this or that?

* Let's play all these things.

Let's play all these things together!

* Repeat

3 Use these or those. Sing another song.

Which ... ,
These ...?

6

th **(2)**

4 🎧 31 Listen, point, and repeat.

1

thick

2

thin

3

think

4

third

5

thirsty

6

thirteen

5  Listen and read.

Three thin monkeys think of three thick sandwiches.

6 What do these thirsty monkeys think of? Draw and say another sentence.

Review 3

1 🎧₃₃ 💡 **Play the game in pairs. Say the words. Complete the chart.**

FINISH

th(2,

th(1)

START

ch

ch	
chair	

sh	
shelf	

th(1)	
this	

th(2)	
thin	

7 wh

1 🎧34 Listen, point, and repeat.

1

wh**at**

2

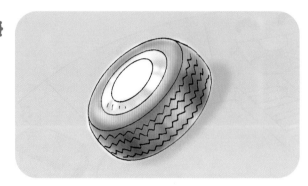

wh**eel**

3

wh**en**

4

wh**ere**

5

wh**ich**

6

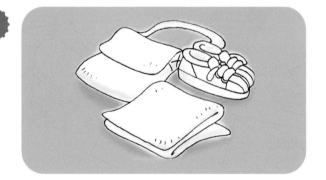

wh**ite**

2 Listen. Then say.

Do you know where to go,
What to do and what to say?
Do you know when it's time to go away?

Yes, I know where to go,
What to do and what to say.
Yes, I know when it's time to go away.

3 Act out the chant.

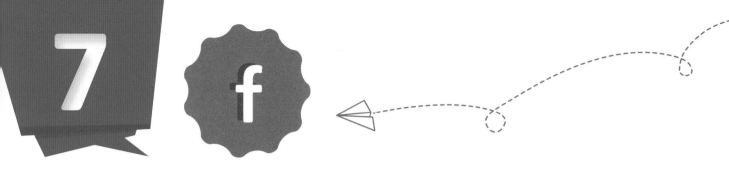

7   f

4 🎧 36   Listen, point, and repeat.

1 fan

2 face

3 fat

4 fish

5 free

6 fork

5  Listen. Then say.

Five fat fish swim in the sea.

A boy with a net is fishing.

"Don't catch us!

We want to be free,"

Say the five fat fish in the sea.

6 Act out the chant.

8   s   sh

1

see

2

she

3

sell

4

shell

5

Sue

6

shoe

2  Listen and read.

Sue can see a rainbow.

She puts on her shoes.

She runs as fast as she can.

What can she find at the end of the rainbow?

Sue can find ...

3 Act out the story.

8   j   ch

4 🎧 40 Listen, point, and repeat.

1

jeep

2

cheap

3

juice

4

choose

5

Jerry

6

cherry

5  Listen. Then say.

Orange juice, apple juice,
Which will you choose?
Mango juice, pear juice,
I just can't choose!

6 Use the names of other juices.
Say another chant.

Review 4

wh

1 🎧42 Say the words.

 1
pan
pen

2
ten
leg

3
dig
dog

4
hot
hut

5
cap
top

6
box
fox

7
shoe
you

8
dog
jog

9
cherry
Jerry

10
hut
shut

11
fat
that

12
pin
thin

13
there
where

14
free
three

15
sell
shell

16
choose
juice

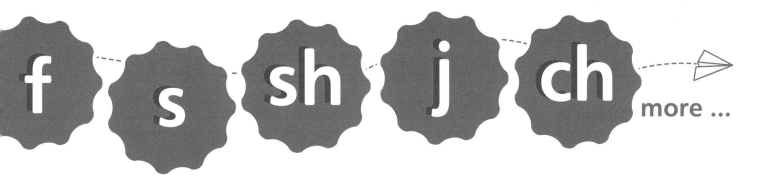

2 Choose and write sixteen words. Play *Bingo*.

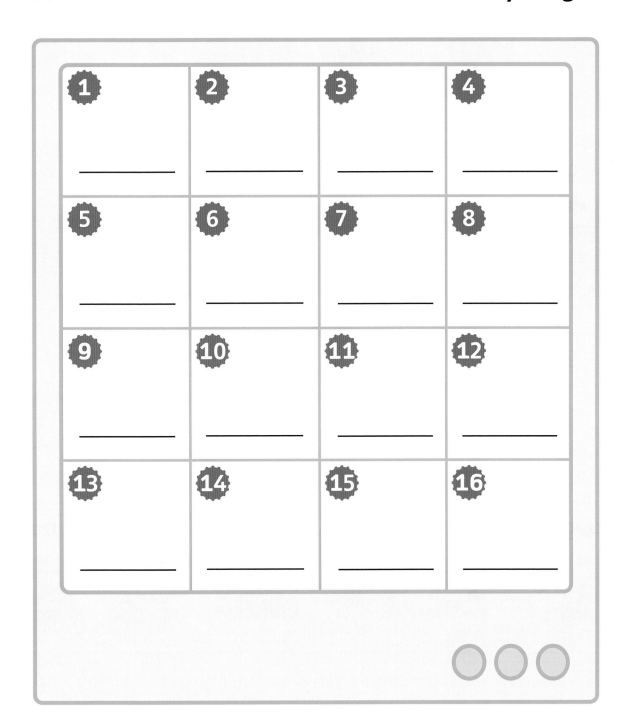

1	2	3	4
5	6	7	8
9	10	11	12
13	14	15	16

PHONICS DICTIONARY

a   man   pan   cap   clap   cat   mat

e   leg   peg   pen   ten   pet   wet

i   big   dig   bin   sing   hit   sit

o   dog   jog   shop   top   hot   pot

u mug rug run sun cut nut

x box relax fox six ax taxi

j jeans jog jump jacket jelly jungle

y year yes you young yellow yo-yo

PHONICS DICTIONARY

 ch

chair	cheese	chips	cherry	chicken	chili

sh

she	shelf	shirt	shark	short	shut

th (1)

this	that	these	those	there	they

th (2)

thick	thin	think	third	thirsty	thirteen

wh

what	**wh**eel	**wh**en	**wh**ere	**wh**ich	**wh**ite

f

fan	**f**ace	**f**at	**f**ish	**f**ree	**f**ork

s
sh

see	**sh**e	**s**ell	**sh**ell	**S**ue	**sh**oe

j
ch

jeep	**ch**eap	**j**uice	**ch**oose	**J**erry	**ch**erry

Pearson Education Limited
KAO TWO
KAO Park
Hockham Way
Harlow, Essex
CM17 9SR
England
and Associated Companies throughout the world.

english.com/englishcode

Authorized Licenced Edition from the English language edition, entitled Phonics Fun, 1st edition published Pearson Education Asia Limited, Hong Kong and Longman Asia ELT © 2003.

This Edition © Pearson Education Limited 2021

First published 2021

ISBN: 978-1-292-32254-4

Sixth impression 2025

Set in Heinemann Roman 17/19pt

Printed in Slovakia by Neografia

Illustrated by Christos Skaltsas (Hyphen S.A.)